T0208686

Contents

FOOD NAMES

Graton- The little bits and pieces scraped from the bottom of the pan after you brown your meat. Used to flavor and color your dish before finishing or making gravy.

Pesto- A sauce used as a spice to enhance the flavor of your dishes. Mix in a blender ¼ cup olive oil with your favorite herb, {exp- parsley, basil, cilantro, or rosemary} with garlic, salt, pepper, and or chives and chop while adding another ¾ cup oil until desired thickness.

Ceviche- raw meat or fish with lemon, olive oil and sometimes balsamic vinegar.

Sava yon- a white wine butter sauce.

Consume- a beef stock used for simmering, boiling, and or flavoring meat dishes.

Sorbet'- French style ice cream with more cream and less air than regular ice cream.

Béarnaise Sauce- egg and butter sauce with white wine or champagne, salt, pepper, and tarragon.

Chimicanga- a vegetable topping for many dishes. In a skillet add a couple ounces EVOO and your favorite vegetable medley, garlic, celery, onion, salt and pepper. Simmer for 5 minutes covered.

Roille- an enriched mayonnaise. Use your favorite spices or herbs to plain mayonnaise.

Remalade- A stuffing for meat or fish, made of cheese, salt and pepper with mayonnaise or ketchup and oil.

Benine- a small desert cake. Used to make Napoleons, short cake or used with meal for texture.

Blinis- a Russian pancake similar to a crepe, it has a leavening agent were crepes do not.

Pasta Fagoli- an Italian bean and pasta soup.

Ossobuco- a beef, pork, or lamb and vegetable dish slow roasted 1 ½ to 2 hours in a red wine and spiced sauce.

Gazpacho- a cold tomato or vegetable soup.

Hamachi- Japanesse for Yellowtail Snapper fish.

Comfit- meat cooked in duck fat.

Compote- a berry or fruit sauce or topping.

Bouillabaisse- a fish, shrimp, clam, and mussel soup.

Cru do- bread baked with cheese and fruit salsa.

Tartar- raw meat with lemon juice and seasonings.

Panzanella- a bread, vegetable, and vinaigrette salad.

Crème Fresh- a cream cheese, yogurt and sugar topping.

Sweet Bread- the thalamus gland in the neck of a cow.

Squab- a young pigeon.

Coulis- pureed fruit in crème fresh.

Mousse- a chocolate, crème fresh, espresso, butter, rum, and gelatin desert.

Panta Vush- Italian for French toast.

Joule- French for jelly or preserves.

Gravlox- thin cut salt cured fish.

Mascapone- an Italian light creamy cheese.

Ratatouille- Eggplant, tomato, onion, and fennel medley, all cooked and spiced separately and served together.

Aioli- a lime and oil sauce.

Galete- a free form tart.

Carpachio- a raw, thin sliced, marinated meat.

Francetta- French smoke cured bacon.

Panchetta- Italian sugar cured bacon.

Gnosh- Chocolate melted and thinned with heavy cream.

Bechamel- a butter and flour "Mother Sauce" used as a basis for 5 other sauces.

Moule- a Mexican sauce used to sweeten or spice a dish.

Marepa- a sautéed base of onions, celery, and carrots.

Trinity- a sautéed base of onions, celery, and tomatoes.

Tempanod- pureed white bean or olive seasoned topping.

Chifinod- rolled, thin cut herbs. Fresh oregano, parsley, basil, or cilantro.

Julianne- long, thin, slice cut products. Carrots, potatoes, peppers

Brunoise- julianne slices chopped to 1/8" cubes.

Zepole- fruit filled flaky pastry.

Fracata bread- spiced pizza dough bread.

Carpachio- quick seared rare centered meat.

Freco- fried flat cheese.

Marmalotta- Italian for marmalade.

Prosciutto bacon- Italian salt and air cured bacon.

Chutne- chopped raw vegetable or fruit topping.

Tompinade- a cheese, anchovy, shallots, and black olive topping.

Brandide- a fish and cheese spiced dip.

Pancotta- bread soup.

Bracoile- browned and seasoned flank steak, breaded, rolled and braised in tomato sauce.

Linguiso- Clams and sausage simmered in onion, garlic, celery, carrots, and tomato strained sauce, topped with sweet onion and grilled pepper relish.

Genoise- 2 layer cake with fruit or vanilla cream filling with Gnosh topping.

Focaccia- unleavened Italian flat bread for adding toppings to.

Frittata- an Italian baked omelet with ingredients like tomato-herb, bacon-mushroom, or potato-onion.

Fegatelli- Pork liver.

Porchetta- roasted whole pig.

Baccala- dried Cod fish.

Cioppino- an Italian seafood stew.

Pollo- Spanish for chicken.

Minestra- greens and beans.

Spinaci- Spinach.

Cavolfiore- Cauliflower.

Chipolle- Onions.

Cucciddata- Italian raisin, fig, and walnut filled cookies.

Bitinibitie- Italian raisin and nut filled pastries.

Biscotti- Italian breakfast cake for coffee dipping.

Biscotto- Italian cake.

Cannoli- Italian creamy cheese filled dessert pastry.

Pagnolata- ethnic Italian honey cluster dessert.

Piapina- an Italian griddled flat bread.

Pagnotta- Italian sweet raisin bread.

Sciachatta- an Italian center filled bread.

Crescia- an Italian "Easter" cheese bread.

Brignolatta- Italian sausage rolls.

Zeppole- Italian flour and potato bread.

Pansotti- Italian pyramid shaped ravioli.

Panna Cotta- a cold pudding dessert.

Gellato- Italian ice cream with less cream.

Risotto- a flavored rice dish. {exp} mushroom, or split pea.

Gnocchi- an Italian potato, egg and flour pasta like dish.

Arancini- Italian rice balls.

Polenta- Italian corn meal dish.

Polpettine- Italian meat balls.

Braciolone- Italian stuffed and rolled beef.

Fegato- calf liver.

Cassatelle- fried ricotta filled triangle ravioli.

Pizzelle- Italian waffle cookies.

Panzoti- an Italian bread salad.

Panelle- an Italian fried chickpea flour pastry.

Sfingi- Sicilian cream puffs.

Serachi- an Asian spicy tomato and pepper sauce.

Wasabi- a Japanese hot horse radish sauce.

Chorizo- a Latin spiced pork sausage.

Tortilla- a corn or flour flat cooked patty used as a wrap or bread.

Guacamole- an avocado spiced spread or dip.

Ibarra chocolate- a spicy Mexican chocolate.

Fajita- chicken or beef with green, red, and yellow peppers, wrapped in a flour tortilla.

Burrito- beef, bean, or chicken and rice or cheese in a folded tortilla.

Enchilada- a beef or chicken and cheese filled rolled tortilla with green pepper salsa topping.

Arroz- Spanish for rice.

Arroz Com Poyo- a Spanish chicken and yellow rice dish.

Pico de Gallo- fresh diced tomato and pepper salsa.

Rajas- creamy poblano pepper strips.

Jicama root- a carrot like tuber vegetable.

Fennel- used as the stalks and tops or the ball shaped tuber root for flavoring.

HERBS

Herbs- used for flavoring and texture in food preparation.

Parsley- a leafy herb used for flavor, aroma, and used whole or chopped as a garnish in many dishes, it adds great taste to soups, salads, meats, mashed potatoes, omelets, and pasta sauces.

Thyme- a small leaf on a stem, you can use whole or strip the leaf off and chop fine. Popular in Mediterranean and French cooking, added to gumbo, seafood, rice and vegetable dishes, it brings a Creole flavor.

Basil- found in most Italian and French recipes, it is used to enliven flavor, and is versatile in egg and seafood dishes, and pasta sauces.

Bay leaves- a leaf from the laurel tree, this herb is used as an essential ingredient in tomato sauces, stews, soups, and in chicken and beef dishes.

Oregano- adds a bold flavor and aroma to Mediterranean, Italian, Southwestern, and Mexican dishes for meat, pasta sauces, and salad dressings. Add a pinch to vegetables, on pizza, in lasagna, or tortilla soup.

Dill Weed- adds a fresh aroma and taste to marinades, seafood, vegetables, pasta, cold soups, and omelets.

Cilantro- with a hint of citrus and anise, it enhances Mexican, Asian, and Indian food. Add to curry or after cooking to stir fry, guacamole or salsa.

Rosemary- teams well with meat, chicken, and many vegetables. Used liberally this aromatic pine like flavor ads pep to rice, soup, potato gratins, eggs and tomato sauces.

Sage- strong flavored, used in poultry stuffing's, on meat, lamb, green beans, and tomato based sauces. Add to soft butter for grilled seafood or as a rub on poultry and wild game.

Tarragon-enhances beef, poultry, seafood, marinades, soups, and egg dishes with a little anise flavor. An essential herb in French cooking.

Lemon grass- used in Asian dishes, it ads a little citrus hint to fish, stir fry, soups, and in marinades for grilled foods.

Mint- with a strong sweet taste, this herb is great in salads, marinades, and as a garnish.

S P I C E S

Spices- used to flavor foods or add color.

Salt- mined underground, or dried from sea water. White iodized, Kosher, or Sea salt from around the worlds oceans, this spice, an essential nutrient, works well with everything.

Pepper- ground from Black, Red, or White peppercorn seeds, this spice is one of the most widely used.

Nutmeg- ground or in nut form, this spice brings a savory flavor to mash potatoes, vegetables, and egg and cheese dishes. Grind some fresh into your coffee or hot chocolate.

Saffron- an expensive, yellowish-red string spice, it imparts a smoky flavor to tomato sauces, bouillabaisse, paellas, and risottos. Picked by hand, this flower stamen costs $500 a pound.

Cinnamon- a tree bark, this spice is perfect for sweet comfort foods, baked goods, meat and poultry dishes, and hot candies. A main ingredient in Curry and Garam Masala.

Star anise- like anise seed, it brings a citrus and cider, along with licorice mellow taste to stews and soups.

Allspice- rich in flavor like clove, it ads a warm flavor and works great in fruit pies, cakes and jams. Add to curries, seafood, meat marinades, and wild game.

Aniseed- has a lightly sweet and licorice taste, it is used in traditional cookies, cakes, and breads. This common Middle Eastern and Indian ingredient, when crushed, brings full flavor to meat dishes.

Caraway Seeds- creating a strong aroma when used in vegetable and fruit recipes, it brings a lemony hint, when used in breads, rolls, and cakes for a snappy flavor.

Cardamom- in pod form, they are great for barbecue sauces, and pickle recipes. When crushed, they are full of little aromatic black seeds good for sweet potatoes and curry dishes. Ground they add subtle flavor to baked goods.

Cayenne pepper- this fiery pepper ads a snappy taste to deviled eggs, egg salad, sauces and soufflés. Used a lot in Mexican and Southwestern dishes, just a pinch is all you need.

Cloves- used whole to stuff into beef or ham, or drop in coffee or tea to add a rich taste. Ground for cakes, stewed fruits, or wild game marinades.

Chives- with a sweet onion and lite garlic taste, it is used on potatoes with sour cream, cream sauces and soups. Add to lemon zest and butter for grilled seafood and meats. Also considered an herb.

Coriander seed- used in Moroccan and Indian dishes, it ads a hint of orange flavor to savory and sweet food when added to cocktail sauce, fruit salad, and summer squash. It is also ground to make one of the ingredients in curry powder.

Cumin- like coriander seeds, it is widely used in Moroccan, Indian, and Mexican dishes. A main ingredient in Garam Masala and Curry dishes it brings a savory flavor to meat and vegetables and works great in chili con carne.

Curry powder- the classic "Indian" spice, this tangy ingredient brings big flavor to chicken, rice, fish, and vegetable dishes. Made with ground coriander seed, cumin, mustard flour, cayenne and black pepper, allspice, tumeric, fennel, fenugreek, and ginger root.

Garlic- a sectioned tuber, it is used in almost any recipe. Whole chopped, and powdered, it brings a pungent taste to meats, seafood, poultry, marinades, and sauces.

Garam Masala- another classic "Indian" spice, it is made from coriander seed, cumin, mustard seed, black peppercorn seed, fenugreek, whole cloves, cardamom pods and whole cinnamon stick that's toasted to release the natural oils, then ground to a fine powder.

Ginger- a tuber root, used in Indian, Asian, Arabian, and Western dishes. Chopped, shredded, or dried and powered, this sweet and hot spice makes a great rub for chicken or beef and is great when added to cakes, cookies, pumpkin pie, and vegetable stir fry.

Juniper berries- with a spicy sweet hint of pine, it is used for poultry and wild game marinades and brines, stuffing's and cabbage dishes. Crush to release its full flavor.

Lemon grass- used mostly in Thai, Malaysian, and Vietnamese cooking, it has a lite citrus flavor in soups, on steamed fish, stir fry, grilled foods, and as a dry rub on poultry.

Marjoram- with a hint of mint, it is great on poultry, fish, ham, and in dishes with tomato and vegetable dishes.

Mulling spice- for an intense and warming flavor, add to wine, hot cider or chocolate drinks. Made from cinnamon, allspice, orange peel, and cloves.

Brown mustard seeds- with a hot and aromatic flavor, it is used in a lot of Indian cuisine. Ground and added to salads and grilled fish and meat dishes for zest. Add to soft butter for seafood or crushed to meat and wine sauces.

Onion- fresh chopped, sautéed, or granulated a great ingredient for comfort foods. Add as a seasoning or rub for sauces, soups, and meat and poultry dishes.

Paprika- with a rich aroma and sweet flavor, add to soups, sauces, meat, poultry, fish wild game, and vegetable dishes, Originally from Hungary, it is made from a lite sweet pepper and is also available in a smoked variety.

Pickling spice- a traditional blend for meats, vegetables, relishes, when poaching seafood, and is essential in beef brisket. Made with chilies, coriander, cumin, ginger, black pepper, allspice, tumeric, cloves, cinnamon, yellow and brown mustard, and bay leaves.

Poppy seeds- crunchy with a nutty flavor, used to sprinkle on muffins and cakes before baking, with honey for a spread, or added to a dressing for noodles or rice.

Poultry seasoning- a blend of herbs and spices, it is used as a rub on poultry or a flavoring for stuffing and potato dishes. Made from cumin, ginger, onion, parsley, white peppercorn, and sage.

Sesame seeds- as one of the oldest seasonings, it brings a nutty flavor to rice, noodles, and vegetable dishes. Sprinkle on grilled chicken, salads, or seafood. Use instead of nuts in baked goods, cookies, and pies.

Shallots- fresh or dried, no kitchen should be without this great little onion. It brings a lite onion and garlic flavor to meats, chicken, sauces, salad dressings, seafood, and vegetables.

Tarragon- essential in French sauces, it brings a subtle anise flavor to beef, poultry, seafood, and vegetables.

Tumeric- it brings a bright golden color to chicken, seafood, vegetables, rice, eggs, and creamy soups. An ingredient in curries and Indian foods.

Vanilla- whole bean or extract, its aroma brings a sweet flavor to ice cream, custard and desserts, baked goods and creamy sauces. Add to a pot of coffee grounds for a great French roast taste.

O

I

L

S

Oils- used to sauté, fry, baste and used as an ingredient in most recipes, baking, salad dressings, and marinades.

Vegetable- an old staple, high in fat and cholesterol, and not as widely used in today's kitchens.

Corn- made from dried and ground kernels, it is slightly lower in fat and cholesterol. Also used to make Ethanol fuel.

Olive- made from the pitted and mashed fruit; most are blended from many different varieties. Raw, Virgin, and Extra Virgin-{EVOO}.

Peanut- made from the roasted and ground nuts; it is very low in fat and cholesterol.

Sunflower- extracted from the dried seed pulp, this oil has "no" fat or cholesterol.

Soy bean- used by commercial companies as a lubricant, and by food manufactures in food recipes. It is fat and cholesterol free.

Grape seed- made from a mix of different varieties, this oil is used a lot in Indian recipes for its low smoke high heat value.

Sesame- extracted from the seeds, this oil is a favorite in Asian stir fry cooking for its flavoring.

Truffle- the most expensive of all oils, it is extracted from the mushrooms and most are mixed with olive oil to extend the use for the general public.

Canola- ground from "rapeseed", this oil is found in many food products we eat today. Low in fat it and with "omega 3 fatty acid", it is one of the healthiest oils on the market.

Palm oil- extracted from the "African" oil palm seed, this oil was widely used in West Africa, Southeast Asia, and Brazil.

Rice bran oil- extracted from the germ and the inner husk, this oil has a high smoke point and is a favorite of several Asian countries for deep and stir frying.

P

A

S

T

A

Pasta- falsely thought to have been brought to Europe from China by Marco Polo, pasta is one of the world's staple foods. Made with flour, eggs, and water, it's boiled and covered by sauce most of the time.

Penne- a small tube pasta with angle cut ends.

Ziti- a medium size tube pasta with square cut ends.

Rigatoni- a large tube pasta with square cut ends.

Spaghetti- a round pasta string, angel hair is smaller.

Linguine- a flat strip pasta, it size varies in size from 1/8" to ½" wide.

Elbow- extruded from a machine and cut to different lengths, this pasta is one of the most widely used.

Lasagna- a flat sheet pasta with rippled edges.

Bow tie- shaped like a bow tie, it comes in three different sizes. Small, medium, and large.

MUSHROOMS

Mushrooms- a fungus,{edible} sautéed, baked, or grilled. Sliced or chopped, they make a great flavoring and side dish.

Chanterelle- with a mildly nutty flavor, this mushroom works great with vegetarian, fish, and fowl dishes when sautéed slowly in butter. Growing in the western "US", and around the world, they are found wild in evergreen [pine] forests.

Morel- brown in color and cone shaped with wrinkles on the outside. Baked, fried, breaded, stewed, creamed, stuffed, or sautéed in butter to release its delicate flavor.

Shitake- an East Asian grown mushroom, they are featured in many Japanese, Thai, Chinese, and Korean cooking, they are used in fancy dishes.

Porcini- also known as a {King Bolete}, they are highly prized around the world. Growing wild in the western "US" in pine forests, when sautéed or fried in butter or oil, it has a mild nutty taste.

Oyster- fan fluted caps ranging from brown to grey, they are used raw or sautéed and have a slight oyster or seafood flavor.

Portabello- a small white button like mushroom, they are the most common and commercially grown and used on the market.

Enoki- known as the Golden Needle, they are a thin white mushroom used in Asian cuisine in Japan and Korea. Used for soups and salads, they have a crisp texture.

Maitaki- also known as "Hen of the woods", native to Japan and North America, this variety is prized in China and Japan for its medicinal properties and taste.

Truffle- grown and hunted in Europe in the wild, white or black, prized for their taste, they are the most expensive mushrooms available in the world.

MARINADES

Marinades- used for flavoring meats, poultry, and fish before cooking.

For Meat- lightly score or poke holes in the surface, then add to marinade and refrigerate for 2 to 12 hours. Grill, pan fry, or bake to your taste.

Chimichurri- puree a red onion, garlic. Chop parsley, cilantro, oregano, red pepper and add olive oil and vinegar.

Balsamic- combine finely chopped red onion, garlic, and rosemary, salt, pepper, olive oil, and balsamic vinegar.

Chipotle and Lime- mince a red onion and garlic cloves, and a mashed chipotle pepper in sauce. Add lime juice, olive oil, honey, salt and pepper.

When baking or frying, don't forget the "Graton", for a flavorful gravy.

For Shrimp- stir fry, bake, sautéed, or grill, refrigerate in marinade for 15 to 30 minutes. When grilling, place shrimp close together on the skewer to prevent curling.

Fireball- finely chop or mince a sweet onion, garlic and parsley. Add melted butter, hot pepper sauce, salt and pepper.

Coconut and Curry- finely chop or mince a sweet onion, and garlic. Add coconut milk, green curry paste or yellow curry powder, salt and pepper.

Hawaiian- mince some garlic, add pineapple juice, teriyaki sauce, cayenne pepper, salt and pepper.

You can use the remaining marinade by sautéing it at a light boil to use as a dipping sauce for your shrimp.

For Pork- marinades work best with natural, not "enhanced" meat that adds salt and water and sodium phosphate. Refrigerate in marinade 2 to 12 hours. Grill, bake, or pan fry.

Zesty Beer- mince garlic and scallions. Add dark beer, vegetable oil, red wine vinegar, whole grain mustard, honey, salt and pepper.

Sweet Cider- mince sweet onion and garlic. Add apple cider, apple cider vinegar, vegetable oil, light brown sugar, and fresh sage.

Orange and Fennel- puree shallots with orange juice, olive oil, white wine vinegar, fresh tarragon, fennel seeds, and orange zest.

Apricot marmalade- salt and pepper your meat and coat with a marmalade and orange juice mix.

When baking or pan frying, don't forget the graton for gravy.

For Chicken- to grill, split bird by cutting down both sides of the backbone and remove to lay flat. Marinate whole or in separate pieces in a bag. Refrigerate in marinade 2 to 12 hours. Bake, fry or grill.

Margarita- mince or finely chop red onion, garlic, and cilantro. Add fresh lime juice, tequila, olive oil, and lime zest. Season with salt and pepper to taste.

Jamaican Jerk- puree scallions, habanero pepper, garlic, fresh thyme, and ginger adding vegetable oil, white vinegar, and allspice for a smooth mix. Season with salt and pepper to taste.

Teriyaki- mince garlic and fresh ginger root. Add honey, soy sauce, vegetable oil, white wine vinegar or pineapple juice. Season with salt and pepper to taste.

Remember to discard used marinade. Do Not Reuse.

For Lamb- when grilling, lamb has a high fat content and is prone to flare ups. Brown both sides over the burner, the move to a lower setting or indirect heat area of the grill. For baking, brown both sides in a skillet before placing in the oven. Refrigerate in marinade 2 to 12 hours.

Greek- mince red onion and garlic. Add yogurt, lemon zest and juice, olive oil, fresh chopped oregano and thyme. Season with salt and pepper to taste.

Tandoori- mince garlic and chop scallions. Add lemon juice, curry powder, olive oil, plain yogurt, and cayenne pepper. Season with salt and pepper to taste.

Pomegranate- mince garlic and chop fresh oregano and mint. Add lemon juice, honey, pomegranate juice and cinnamon. Season with salt and pepper to taste.

You can use the remaining marinade with the "graton" by simmering at a slow boil for a great sauce.

Fish- bake, pan or deep fry, or grill using a fine mesh aluminum plate, or aluminum foil adding potatoes, vegetables, and a little water to make a closed steamer. Refrigerate marinated fish for 15 to 30 minutes.

Moroccan- chop cilantro, parsley, and mint. Add lemon juice, olive oil, powered garlic, paprika, ground cumin, and cayenne pepper. Season with salt and pepper to taste.

Dijon- mince garlic and chop fresh tarragon. Add white wine vinegar, olive oil, and Dijon mustard. Season with salt and pepper to taste.

Lemon Pepper- mince shallots. Add lemon juice and zest, olive oil, Dijon mustard, soy sauce, and sugar. Season with salt and pepper to taste.

When planning to use marinade as a dipping sauce, remember to keep a little out before adding fish to avoid cross contamination of raw fish. You can also simmer to reduce.

F

L

O

U

R

S

Flours- a powder ground from grains, seeds, or roots, it is a staple food and main ingredient in baked goods and used as a coating for meat and fish. A starch [carbohydrate], some recipes require a leavening agent to produce a light and soft product.

Processed White- made from the bran and endosperm of the wheat kernel and bleached, it is the highest in carbohydrates and is the most widely used in the world.

Whole Wheat- ground from the bran, endosperm, and germ of the kernel, this flour has fewer carbohydrates and makes a light brown color in baked goods.

Almond flour- made from fine ground almond nuts, this flour is used a lot in the Middle East.

Bean flour- ground from dried or pulverized fresh beans. White, chickpea and others, this flour is used widely in South American and Middle Eastern countries.

Brown Rice flour- ground from the whole dried kernel, this flour is a major staple in South East Asian cuisine and is used to make edible rice paper.

Buckwheat-ground from "Dicot" plant seeds, this wheat is used in the "US" for pancakes, Japan for noodles, and mixed with wheat flour in Russia for blinis.

Cassava- made from the plants root, when purified, this flour forms a perfect starch. Also known as "Tapioca" flour, it is used to make breads, pancakes, pudding, and a porridge called "Fufu".

Chestnut- with either "Perigord or Lunigiana" varieties, it is used in the Mediterranean for breads, cakes, and pastas, and in Italy for desserts. The original "polenta" flour.

Chickpea- also called "Garbanzo beans", and known as "Gram flour", it is a major staple in Indian and Italian cooking.

Chuno- made from many varieties of dried potatoes like "Malanga or Yucca", it is used in many South American and Caribbean countries.

Corn- known as "maize", this flour is called corn meal when ground, and "masa" when finely ground. Used in the "US", Mexico, South America, and called "Makki Ka Atta in India and Pakistan.

Cornstarch- also known as corn flour, it is the powered "endosperm" only from the corn kernel.

Mesquite- made from the dried and ground pods of the mesquite tree, this flour has a sweet and nutty flavor used in a wide variety of foods.

Peasemeal- also called pea meal, it is made from roasted and finely ground yellow peas.

Peanut- made from cooked, dried, and fine ground peanuts, it is high protein alternative flour.

Potato- using the whole tuber, it is cooked, mashed, drum dried, and flaked. It is used widely around the world.

Rye- made from rye grass seed, used exclusively for "Rye" bread, it is also mixed with wheat flour for the traditional sourdough breads of Poland, Germany, and Scandinavia.

Hovis- a wheat germ based flour, used in the "UK" to make bread and bisquits of the same name. A patented flour mix.

Matzah- a white flour used to make an Asian unleavened bread called "chapati" and a Jewish cracker bread for their holidays.

Breads- baked, fried, or griddled, a staple food around the world.

White- made from the bran and endosperm of the wheat kernel and bleached, this is the most common bread and the highest in carbohydrates.

Whole Wheat- made from the whole kernel, but not bleached, this bread is lower in carbohydrates. Most are a light brown in color.

Rye- made from rye seed flour, it requires a starter mix, a baking soda leavening agent, and usually has whole dried seeds in it.

Pumpernickel- made from enriched Wheat, Rye, Barley, and Soy flour with spices, it is a dark Rye bread also called Russian Black.

Roti- a small unleavened whole wheat bread fried on a griddle, with "Chapati" as a larger version in Asia, and "Naan" as a leavened version in India and Pakistan.

Hovis- a wheat germ base with 10% bran flour used to make breads and bisquits in the United Kingdom. A patented flour process.

P

E

P

P

E

R

S

Peppers- This is a list of the most commonly used peppers from around the world. They are rated for how "HOT" they are.

Habanera- a Chinese family pepper grown in South America, this is one of the "HOTTEST" peppers. Small, round, and red when ripe, you don't need much for flavoring. Hot scale-#10.

Pablano- a green "Ancho" pepper, it is a large, pointed sweet pepper usually roasted and peeled for soups, sauces, casseroles, and stuffed with cheese or meats. Hot scale-#2-3.

Ancho- a dried "Pablano", this sweet chili pepper has a hint of raisin and plum. Light brown or black, it is commonly used in Mexico. Hot scale-#4.

Cayenne- one of the "Hottest" chili peppers, this red, 6 to 10 inch long and thin pepper, usually curls on the end. Dried and ground for a popular spice. Hot scale-#8-9.

Charleston Hot- a "hybrid" cayenne pepper, it grows 4 to 5 inches long and is ¾ inch wide and curled to a point, this pepper is twice as "Hot" and changes from green to orange when ripe. Hot scale-#9.5.

Cherry- round red cherry shaped, this pepper is mild to moderately "Hot", and sold fresh or pickled. Hot scale-#1-5.

Chipotle- a smoke roasted "Poblano" popular in Mexican and South Western cooking and packed in "Adobo" sauce, it has a sweet smoky, chocolaty taste.

Fresno- a "hybrid" version of the Jalapeno pepper 3 to 4 inches long, it is red when ripe. Developed in California, it is hotter than its cousin. Hot scale-#7 to 8.

Jalapeno- a 2 to 3 inch pepper sold green, that can be used for flavoring, pickling, or smoke roasted to make "Chipotle" chilies. Hot scale-#5 to 7

Paprika- Hungarian for pepper, it is ground fine for a sweet, warm, and savory spice great for flavoring and coloring foods. Hot scale-#0 to 2.

Pasilla- one of Mexico's best dried chili peppers, called the "Black Pepper" it turns to purple-dark brown when ripe. With a smoky flavor and raisin like aroma, it is great in tamales and quesadillas. Hot scale-#3 to 5.

Pimento- a small heart shaped Spanish pepper, it is not as savory or hot as the Hungarian version. Hot scale-#0.

Pepper Corns- a seed pod of the "Black pepper" vines grown in India; they come in three different styles. Black, White, and Green, they are dried and ground to make the common varieties we use today. Hot scale-#3-4.

Bell Pepper- originally from northern South America, they was brought to Europe by Columbus in 1493. With a sweet and pungent taste, they come in three different colors. Green, Red, and Orange. Hot scale-#0.

Scotch Bonnets- native to the Caribbean, and related to the Habanera, it is almost as hot. With its apply-cherry tomato flavor, a little is great in sauces and salads. Hot scale-#9.5.

Serrano- a native Mexican and South Western mountain grown 1 to 4 inch torpedo shaped pepper, it is commonly used to flavor stews, casseroles, and egg dishes. Hot scale-#6 to 7.

Tabasco- "the" chili pepper used to make "Tabasco brand" hot sauce, this pepper is originally from Mexico. This "HOT" little 1 inch long variety grows upright on its bush and is red when ripe. Hot scale-#9.

SWEETENERS

Natural Sweeteners- used to take the bitterness out, or sweeten bland food and drinks, there are many natural and extracted plant products.

White Sugar- known as "Sucrose", a processed product from either sugar cane stalks or sugar beets. Crushed and strained, the juice is boiled down and dried to make the base product it is processed from.

Cane sugar- the base product from the stalks, it is crushed and the juice is boiled down and left raw to dry.

Sugar Beets- another base product used to make white sugar, this tuber, farmed in the mid-west, has become a more economical and environmentally safer way to obtain sugar.

Brown Sugar- made from raw cane sugar with molasses added, it has a brown color and is used in many recipes.

Molasses- a byproduct of sugar manufacturing, its quality depends on the amount of sugar, and method of extraction.

Sweet Sorghum syrup- made from sorghum grass seed, it was introduced by African slaves in the 17th century and has been grown in the South Western "US" since the 1850s.

Honey-processed from the nectar of flowers naturally by bees, it is collected by bee keepers from their hive boxes, or from wild hives and extracted from the comb.

Barley Sugar- made from regular sugar, barley water, and cream of tartar, it is the basis for a delicious British candy first made by Benedictine Monks of France in 1638. Poured into metal molds, it was used to make "clear toys", a Victorian Christmas treat.

Caramel- made by heating sugar to 370 degrees in a copper pot or pan, the molecules break down and change their consistence to form brown syrup used to make candies, dip apples, and make pralines, nougats, brittles and crème brulees.

Artificial Substitutes- for those people that do not, or can not use regular sugars.

Saccharin- the first substitute, a highly concentrated sulfimide, it has a slight bitter or metallic taste. Banned in Canada in 1977 due to animal research, it has a warning from the FDA to use in small amounts.

Aspartame- a newer sweetener, known by its number [E951] in Europe, it is an ester acid dipeptide. 200 times sweeter than sugar, it can be used is used in frozen desserts, gelatins, beverages, and chewing gum.

Splenda- a "patented" sweetener product made from sugar without the calories, it can be used wherever you use regular sugar.

Truvia, or Via- "patented" sweetener products made from the "Stevia", or sweet leaf plant grown in the southern "US and South America.

S

U

B

S

T

I

T

U

T

E

S

Substitutions- when you don't have a certain ingredient, these will work for most popular foods.

Butter- lard, margarine, vegetable oil, shortening, or rendered bacon fat depending on what you are cooking.

Lard- vegetable shortening or oil, butter, or margarine.

Vegetable oil- olive oil, corn oil, canola oil, shortening, or lard.

Shortening- lard, vegetable oil, low salt butter, or margarine.

White sugar- brown or cane sugar, honey,, caro syrup, or the artificial Aspartame, Saccharine, Splenda, or the products from the "Stevia" plant Truvia-Via.

White Vinegar- add lemon juice to either white wine vinegar, red wine vinegar, or apple cider vinegar if you don't mind adding flavor to the dish.

Balsamic Vinegar- Sherry or cider vinegar.

White Flour- whole wheat, buckwheat, corn, potato, or rice depending on what you are making.

Cheeses- there are many varieties that can be substituted. These are just a few.

Cottage Cheese- Ricotta cheese or farmer cheese.

Goat Cheese- Feta cheese.

Cream Cheese- Ricotta cheese and a little low fat milk whipped together.

Romano Cheese- Parmesan cheese.

Mascarpone Cheese- whipped Cream cheese and low fat milk.

Heavy Cream- Evaporated milk, or sweet milk and butter.

Sour Cream- Sour milk and butter, or Butter milk and vinegar.

Half and Half- whole milk and butter, whole milk and light or heavy cream, or low fat milk and heavy cream.

Sweetened Condensed Milk- non fat dry milk + boiling water + sugar + butter blended smooth, or evaporated milk + sugar simmered on low heat until sugar is dissolved.

Evaporated Milk- Light cream, or non fat dry milk + water whipped until smooth.

Regular [Whole] Milk- Evaporated milk and water.

Low Fat or Skim Milk- non fat dry milk and water.

Yogurt-Sour Cream, Butter milk, or Cottage Cheese whipped smooth.

Chili Oil- Vegetable or Canola oil and a pinch of Cayenne pepper.

Sesame Oil- toast Sesame seeds in vegetable oil.

Capers- chopped green olives.

Celery- Green peppers or fennel root.

Chives- Scallion green tops.

Jicama- Chestnuts or tart apple.

Leeks- Shallots.

Shallots- white part of the Green Onion, or Leeks.

Tomitilla- green Tomato and lemon juice.

Tomato Juice- tomato sauce and water strained through butchers cloth.

Tomato Soup- tomato sauce and water or milk.

Tomato Paste- tomato sauce reduced by ½ to a thick paste.

Beer- apple cider or beef broth.

Coconut Milk- regular milk and sugar.

Honey- apple cider and sugar, or corn syrup.

Ketchup- tomato sauce with sugar and vinegar.

Mayonnaise- cottage cease blended smooth, salad dressing, sour cream, or yogurt.

Tabasco Sauce- tomato juice and cayenne or black pepper.

Tartar Sauce- Mayonnaise and Pickle relish.

Worchestershire Sauce- Soy sauce + Tabasco + Lemon juice + a dash of sugar.

Truffle Mushrooms or Oil- sauté Shitake mushrooms in olive oil.

Fruits- there are many substitutes for different types of fruits.

Raisins- Dates- Figs.

Oranges- Tangerines- Apricots.

Lemons- Limes.

Peaches- Nectarines.

Strawberries- Blueberries- Mulberries [black berries].

Apples- Pears.

Wines- for cooking.

Red Wine- use apple cider, tomato sauce, or beef broth.

White Wine- white grape juice, apple cider, or beef broth.

Rice Wine- dry Sherry.

Wines- for marinades.

Uses above substitutes and add Vinegar, Sugar, and Water.

MEASUREMENT

Measurements- Whether "Liquid" or "Dry", you need to know how to convert from "US" to "Metric" and back.

Liquid- used for all "wet" ingredients. Oils, juices, water, milk, ect.

1 tsp 1/3 tbls 5 mls.

1 tbls ½ oz 3 tsp 15 mls.

2 tsp 1 oz 6 tsp 30 mls.

¼ cup 2 oz 4 tbls 60 mls.

1/3 cup 2 2/3 oz 5 tbls+1tsp 80 mls.

½ cup 4 oz 1 grl 8 tbls 120 mls.

2/3 cup 5 1/3 oz 10 tbls+2tsp 160 mls.

¾ cup 6 oz 12 tbls 180 mls.

7/8 cup 7 oz 14 tbls 210 mls.

1 cup 8 oz ½ pt 16 tbls 240 mls.

2 cups 16 oz 1 pt 32 tbls 475 mls.

4 cups 32 oz 1 qrts 950 mls.

1 litre 1.057 qrts 1000 mls.

4 qrts 128 oz 1 gal 3785 mls.

These numbers are rounded out. When converting for large quantities, consult your cook book or internet.

tsp=teaspoons, tbls=tablespoons

oz=ounce, pt=pint, qrts=quart, gal=gallon, grl=grill

Dry Weights- used for non liquid measurements.

"US" to Metric Conversions

1 oz 30 grams.

2 oz 55 grams

3 oz 85 grams.

4 oz ¼ lb 125 grams.

8 oz ½ lb 240 grams.

12 oz ¾ lb 375 grams.

16 oz 1 lb 454 grams

1 Kilo 2.2 lb 35.2 oz 1000 grams.

These are world wide standard conversions, except for Canadian and Australian which have their own, which varies up or down a little.

Temperature conversion- when watching some of the shows from England and Australia, the "Host" will be using "Metric" temperature settings.

Setting Farenheight Celcius

Low 170 80

225 107

250 121

275 135

Medium 300 149

325 163

350 177

375 191

High 400 204

425 218

450 232

475 246

These are standard "US to metric conversions and can vary from country to country.